Hope that Transforms

Hope that Transforms

Daily readings for Advent and Christmas

CANTERBURY
PRESS
Norwich

© St John's College Nottingham 2006

First published in 2006 by the Canterbury Press Norwich
(a publishing imprint of Hymns Ancient & Modern Limited,
a registered charity)
9–17 St Alban's Place, London N1 0NX

www.scm-canterburypress.co.uk

Scripture quotations are from the New Revised Standard Version of
the Bible, copyright 1989 by the Division of Christian Education of
the National Council of the Churches of Christ in the USA.
Used by permission. All rights reserved.

British Library Cataloguing in Publication data

A catalogue record for this book is available
from the British Library

ISBN 1-85311-784 6/978-1-85311-784-8

Typeset by Regent Typesetting, London
Printed and bound by
MPG Books Ltd, Bodmin, Cornwall

Contents

Introduction

In times of change and uncertainty, we can respond in one of two ways. We can choose to withdraw, retreating back into things we feel certain about, hoping the change will go away. Or we can embrace the time of change as an open door of promise. But if we are to respond this way we need to have confidence in the God of hope, who transforms uncertainty into opportunity. So many things around us point to change, and yet as we approach Christmas we are reminded that God has not left us to face this alone. And Advent is a special time to remember that God will once again visit this his world and make all things new.

The readings in this book are taken from the Revised Common Lectionary, and staff and students at St John's College, Nottingham, offer their own reflections on them. They are offered to encourage you as you face your own uncertainties, that you may discover afresh the hope that transforms.

St John's has been training men and women for a whole range of ministries for over 140 years. The college has often been at the forefront of developing creative new ways of training, and we now train people full time and part time, on mixed mode training (combining study with curacy over five years) and by distance learning, for ordained ministry, youth ministry and a wide variety of lay ministries. For more information, visit our website: www.stjohns-nottm.ac.uk.

The money raised by the sale of this book will go towards our student hardship fund and our development fund, and contribute towards innovations in training for the church of today and the church of tomorrow.

Revd Dr Ian Paul
Dean of Studies

Sunday 26 November

John 6.1–5

After this Jesus went to the other side of the Sea of Galilee, also called the Sea of Tiberias. A large crowd kept following him, because they saw the signs that he was doing for the sick. Jesus went up the mountain and sat down there with his disciples. Now the Passover, the festival of the Jews, was near. When he looked up and saw a large crowd coming towards him, Jesus said to Philip, 'Where are we to buy bread for these people to eat?'

How do you feed a multitude?

Most of my memories about Christmas seem to revolve around food. I had a legion of great-aunts and uncles who all came to us for Christmas Day and Boxing Day, and preparing food for them all seemed to take months. The cake was made in September and iced the first week of December, the pudding was made in October, and the food shopping began in September and went on into December as our freezer and garage filled up in preparation.

Jesus' disciples, on the other hand, are not able to prepare. My mother took over four months to prepare for twenty people but Jesus asks the disciples to produce food for thousands in a matter of seconds. I do not want to think how big the turkey would have needed to be! But I am amazed by the calm way in which Jesus takes the pitiful amount the disciples can find, thanks his Father for it and gives it to the crowd. The Bible does not tell us how the loaves and fish multiplied or exactly when this happened so that everyone had as much as they wanted. What it does demonstrate very clearly is God's ability to provide and his power to do what seems impossible.

At times we can be very poor at trusting Jesus. But the knowledge of what he is able to do should transform our attitude to the situations we face.

Prayer

Jesus, help us to understand
    more of who you are and the power you have.
Give us faith to bring our situations to you
    and to trust you to provide what we need. Amen.

Monday 27 November

Psalm 71.19–24

Your power and your righteousness, O God,
   reach the high heavens.

You who have done great things,
   O God, who is like you?
You who have made me see many troubles and calamities
   will revive me again;
from the depths of the earth
   you will bring me up again.
You will increase my honour,
   and comfort me once again.

I will also praise you with the harp
   for your faithfulness, O my God;
I will sing praises to you with the lyre,
   O Holy One of Israel.
My lips will shout for joy
   when I sing praises to you;
   my soul also, which you have rescued.
All day long my tongue will talk of your righteous help,
for those who tried to do me harm
   have been put to shame, and disgraced.

Who is like God?

How often have you felt exactly like the Psalmist does here? It seems like the whole world is stacked against you and that everyone is talking against you behind your back. Unfortunately, life does sometimes feel like that and however irrational that feeling may be, it can dominate our outlook.

The Psalmist's response to his fears is to turn them over to God. Who, he asks rhetorically, is like God? He knows that in God is his hope and that God can transform his situation. He looks back and recalls to himself how God has been active in his life for as long as he has had that life. Even at birth, God's hand was upon him. When it seems that the world is against us, that all around is working to make life difficult and there is nothing we can do about it, we would do well to follow the Psalmist's lead.

Advent is a time for preparation. As we prepare to celebrate the coming of Christ, this is one way that we can ask him to prepare us for the rest of our lives. It is his desire that we have security in him and look to him for our help. With that in mind, we can pray with the Psalmist:

Do not be far from me, my God;
   come quickly, God, to help me.
                (verse 12)

God is faithful and answers the prayers of his children when they ask. This Advent, if life seems to be conspiring against you, turn to God and ask for help. He longs to return you to the place where, like the Psalmist, your lips will shout for joy.

Tuesday 28 November

Isaiah 40.12–17 and 25–26

Who has measured the waters in the hollow of his hand
    and marked off the heavens with a span,
enclosed the dust of the earth in a measure,
    and weighed the mountains in scales
    and the hills in a balance?
Who has directed the spirit of the LORD,
    or as his counsellor has instructed him?
Whom did he consult for his enlightenment,
    and who taught him the path of justice?
Who taught him knowledge,
    and showed him the way of understanding?
Even the nations are like a drop from a bucket,
    and are accounted as dust on the scales;
    see, he takes up the isles like fine dust.
Lebanon would not provide fuel enough,
    nor are its animals enough for a burnt offering.
All the nations are as nothing before him;
    they are accounted by him as less than nothing and emptiness.

To whom then will you compare me,
    or who is my equal? says the Holy One.
Lift up your eyes on high and see:
    Who created these?
He who brings out their host and numbers them,
    calling them all by name;
because he is great in strength,
    mighty in power,
    not one is missing.

Not one is missing

God's people had been sent into exile in Babylon in 587 BCE. All of us can experience our own form of exile, whether it is the death of a loved one, divorce, redundancy or other traumatic experience. My own experience has been that of divorce. In some strange way I believe that I can empathize with the Israelites of that era – utterly rejected, dejected and alone.

I had joined a divorce support group that was run by our church. I met people in a similar situation, but the feeling of being alone never left me. One of the group commented that we were like a number of individual ships all travelling in our own isolated worlds.

The opportunity then arose for a few of us from the group to meet together to read the Bible. We followed some study notes and entered into discussion about the meaning of what we had read. What we all discovered was that our sense of loneliness disappeared. Even when we were on our own, we no longer had the same sense of isolation. We had discovered something new – the presence of God in our lives! My rejection, dejection and loneliness all evaporated, replaced with a new hope and enjoyment in life.

During the months that followed, we explored various issues within the Bible and discovered a renewed and strengthened faith in God – and found that our zest for life and hope for a future had been returned to us. Because of God's power, Isaiah says, not one of the stars is missing (verse 26). I discovered that I had not gone missing either – God still had hold of me. There was life after divorce after all! The thought that God cared for me personally gave me renewed hope and transformed my life!

Reflection

Next time there is a clear night, go out and look at the stars. Remember that God's power means he will never forget you, never let you go missing.

Wednesday 29 November

Revelation 16.1–12

Then I heard a loud voice from the temple telling the seven angels, 'Go and pour out on the earth the seven bowls of the wrath of God.'

So the first angel went and poured his bowl on the earth, and a foul and painful sore came on those who had the mark of the beast and who worshipped its image.

The second angel poured his bowl into the sea, and it became like the blood of a corpse, and every living thing in the sea died.

The third angel poured his bowl into the rivers and the springs of water, and they became blood. And I heard the angel of the waters say,

'You are just, O Holy One, who are and were,
    for you have judged these things;
because they shed the blood of saints and prophets,
    you have given them blood to drink.
It is what they deserve!'

And I heard the altar respond,

'Yes, O Lord God, the Almighty,
    your judgments are true and just!'

The fourth angel poured his bowl on the sun, and it was allowed to scorch people with fire; they were scorched by the fierce heat, but they cursed the name of God, who had authority over these plagues, and they did not repent and give him glory.

The fifth angel poured his bowl on the throne of the beast, and its kingdom was plunged into darkness; people gnawed their tongues in agony, and cursed the God of heaven because of their pains and sores, and they did not repent of their deeds.

The sixth angel poured his bowl on the great river Euphrates, and its water was dried up in order to prepare the way for the kings from the east.

Until he leads justice to victory

Posters for the film *The Shawshank Redemption* carried the tag-line 'Fear can hold you prisoner; hope can set you free.' Our hope is in the victory that Jesus has won against all brutality and injustice. After a brutal and unjust death upon a cross, the crucified Christ had the last word of victory when he was raised to life and ascended to the right hand of the Father, and he will return as the judge of the whole earth. The message of Revelation is clear: Christ will come again, and when he returns he will judge the world with justice and truth (Revelation 16.7).

A possible backdrop for the book of Revelation is the bloody reign of the Emperor Nero when it is believed that many Christians were publicly tortured and murdered. The book is a rallying cry to the fearful, suffering, persecuted church of Asia Minor (modern-day western Turkey), exhorting them to know that their hope cannot be shattered by violence or death. It is unshakeable and secure for all eternity in the person of the living Lord Jesus Christ. He cares deeply about justice and mercy; no act of human cruelty against another person has evaded his all-seeing eyes, and his heart is not stony or apathetic to the plight of the suffering, oppressed and persecuted. Justice will be done. Hate, suffering, injustice and brutality will cease to exist and instead we shall see Jesus face to face and he will wipe away every tear from our eyes. When we pray 'May your kingdom come, on earth as it is in heaven' this is what we are asking for.

In praying this we are pledging ourselves to fight for justice, to stand firm no matter what the cost, knowing that Jesus has the last word of victory.

Prayer

Lord Jesus Christ, I have placed my hope in you. I trust you. May your kingdom come on earth as in heaven. Thank you that by your cross and resurrection you are victorious against brutality and injustice. Help me today to stand firm no matter what I face, and fight for justice and mercy wherever I am. Come Lord Jesus, come. Amen.

Thursday 30 November

John 12.20–32

Now among those who went up to worship at the festival were some Greeks. They came to Philip, who was from Bethsaida in Galilee, and said to him, 'Sir, we wish to see Jesus.' Philip went and told Andrew; then Andrew and Philip went and told Jesus. Jesus answered them, 'The hour has come for the Son of Man to be glorified. Very truly, I tell you, unless a grain of wheat falls into the earth and dies, it remains just a single grain; but if it dies, it bears much fruit. Those who love their life lose it, and those who hate their life in this world will keep it for eternal life. Whoever serves me must follow me, and where I am, there will my servant be also. Whoever serves me, the Father will honour.

'Now my soul is troubled. And what should I say – "Father, save me from this hour"? No, it is for this reason that I have come to this hour. Father, glorify your name.' Then a voice came from heaven, 'I have glorified it, and I will glorify it again.' The crowd standing there heard it and said that it was thunder. Others said, 'An angel has spoken to him.' Jesus answered, 'This voice has come for your sake, not for mine. Now is the judgement of this world; now the ruler of this world will be driven out. And I, when I am lifted up from the earth, will draw all people to myself.'

Reflected glory

On a summer's evening, a friend and I went for a walk up to the top of a nearby hill. The path was winding and occasionally enclosed by big old trees. Once we reached the summit, we laid out a blanket, sat down and looked at the beautiful view in front of us. But as the darkness drew over, we realized that we did not have a torch to see our way back down the path. As the sun set and the light quickly faded, we began to make our way back down the hill. Surprisingly, there was enough light for us to make the journey – light provided by the moon. The soft moonlight on a clear night gave enough light for our way to be safe and clear.

It was only later, as I reflected on what could have been a treacherous return journey, that I was struck by the power of that seemingly soft moonlight. It is truly amazing that the moon itself provides no light at all – it merely reflects the light of the sun. We never doubt the ability of the sun to rise each morning and give light to the daytime, and even though it goes away at night, we continue to believe it will light the world again each day. Of course, the sun does not disappear, but continues to shine out light on other parts of the world and on the moon.

In this passage from John, Jesus tells us to 'walk in the light' and to 'believe in the light' in order that we might be 'children of the light'. As the ultimate light in the darkness of this world, Jesus knew that his followers too could be reflections of his light despite that darkness. Just as the sun never stops radiating light, Jesus continues to shine in our lives – and if we choose to be his reflections in the world, we can light up the path for others.

Reflection

Do you feel you reflect the light of Jesus in your life? Why?

Pray for someone you know who needs to know the light, and consider how you might be a 'moon', reflecting the 'sunlight' of Jesus.

Friday 1 December

Psalm 139.1–10, 23–24

O LORD, you have searched me and known me.
You know when I sit down and when I rise up;
   you discern my thoughts from far away.
You search out my path and my lying down,
   and are acquainted with all my ways.
Even before a word is on my tongue,
   O LORD, you know it completely.
You hem me in, behind and before,
   and lay your hand upon me.
Such knowledge is too wonderful for me;
   it is so high that I cannot attain it.

Where can I go from your spirit?
   Or where can I flee from your presence?
If I ascend to heaven, you are there;
   if I make my bed in Sheol, you are there.
If I take the wings of the morning
   and settle at the farthest limits of the sea,
even there your hand shall lead me,
   and your right hand shall hold me fast.

Search me, O God, and know my heart;
   test me and know my thoughts.
See if there is any wicked way in me,
   and lead me in the way everlasting.

O come, O come Immanuel

My favourite Advent hymn expresses our deepest longing for Christ to come and transform our lives and our world, our longing for his return in glory to reign completely unhindered for eternity.

This is one of my favourite Psalms because it expresses the intimacy of an all-present, all-knowing God. We cannot escape his presence; in the highs and lows he is there. Before our birth he knew us; he knows when we sit, our next word, our next thought – he knows us!

I regularly come back to this Psalm as it expresses the closeness of God in contrast to a society that is searching for intimacy in all the wrong places. God is not a distant God, impassive or uncaring.

Advent asks us to prepare our hearts for Immanuel, God with us, a living, breathing, hurting, laughing, real, with-skin-on, radical God in the person of Jesus Christ, and welcome the awesome difference he can make to our lives and in our world.

This is our God; he knows what it is to be human; he understands us. He knows the good, the bad and the ugly about us *and* he loves us, accepts us and invites us into a transforming relationship with him. How I long for others in my family and in our world to know this radical love and acceptance, to know the hope that God *is* with us, at all times, in all circumstances, and that one day he will come in a new way and truly transform this hurting world.

Reflection

This Advent, can we be truly radical and pray verses 23 and 24 of this Psalm, asking God to search our heart? Do we long for Immanuel to come and transform us, that we might take his love and acceptance to others, to transform our hurting world in his power, till his kingdom comes?

Saturday 2 December

Isaiah 42.10–17

Sing to the LORD a new song,
  his praise from the end of the earth!
Let the sea roar and all that fills it,
  the coastlands and their inhabitants.
Let the desert and its towns lift up their voice,
  the villages that Kedar inhabits;
let the inhabitants of Sela sing for joy,
  let them shout from the tops of the mountains.
Let them give glory to the LORD,
  and declare his praise in the coastlands.
The LORD goes forth like a soldier,
  like a warrior he stirs up his fury;
he cries out, he shouts aloud,
  he shows himself mighty against his foes.

For a long time I have held my peace,
  I have kept still and restrained myself;
now I will cry out like a woman in labour,
  I will gasp and pant.
I will lay waste mountains and hills,
  and dry up all their herbage;
I will turn the rivers into islands,
  and dry up the pools.
I will lead the blind
  by a road they do not know,
by paths they have not known
  I will guide them.
I will turn the darkness before them into light,
  the rough places into level ground.
These are the things I will do,
  and I will not forsake them.
They shall be turned back and utterly put to shame –
  those who trust in carved images,
who say to cast images,
  'You are our gods.'

If the world does not need a Saviour

In the summer box office hit *Superman Returns*, there is a particular scene where Superman takes Lois Lane into the Earth's upper atmosphere and hovers there surveying the world below. Against a backdrop of a billion stars he proclaims, 'You wrote that the world doesn't need a saviour, but every day I hear them crying for one.'

This remarkable scene allows us to address two related thoughts. The first is that no matter how independent our communities may seem, no matter how self-sufficient they try to portray themselves, deep inside there is a desire to connect with the God who has placed eternity in their heart – communities crying out for a Saviour.

The second is that we often think that our Saviour is looking down at his world and hearing the cries of his people. In this, we would be only half right. We do indeed serve a God who hears the cries of his people, but we do not serve a God who simply looks down from heaven and listens. If the incarnation teaches us anything, it is that God does not solve all earth's problems from a heavenly control room. Our Saviour walks with his people; he touches the hurting, befriends the lonely, and frees those who have become captive to their own selfish desires. Today's readings show us a great Saviour who chooses through his great love to be active in the affairs of humanity.

Our purpose this Christmas is simple. We must look at our community for the signs of where our Saviour is at work, and when we see them, we must roll up our sleeves and get involved.

Our world still needs a Saviour.

Prayer

Father, open my eyes that I may see where you are already working in my community. Open my heart so that I may not just see but be motivated into action. Allow me to show your world the Saviour they are crying out for this Christmas. Amen.

Sunday 3 December

Romans 13.11–14

Besides this, you know what time it is, how it is now the moment for you to wake from sleep. For salvation is nearer to us now than when we became believers; the night is far gone, the day is near. Let us then lay aside the works of darkness and put on the armour of light; let us live honourably as in the day, not in revelling and drunkenness, not in debauchery and licentiousness, not in quarrelling and jealousy. Instead, put on the Lord Jesus Christ, and make no provision for the flesh, to gratify its desires.

Ordering our lives

Our children love playing cards. They love to sort the pack out (they are just learning how to shuffle), recruit some fellow players, set the game up, and see who wins. I am sure this is good educationally – but the most important thing is that we have great fun together.

Interestingly, the one thing they never tire of is putting the cards in order. There seems to be something deeply satisfying about having each suit in its place, with all the cards from ace to king following in turn.

In Paul's letters, and especially in his letter to the Romans, he too likes to get things in the right order. The first part of the letter, from chapter 1 all the way to chapter 11, sets out the wonderful things God has done in Christ for us and for our salvation – redeeming us from sin (3.24), pouring his love into our hearts by his Spirit (5.5), enabling us to cry out to him as Father (8.15) and much more besides. The second part of the letter turns on a great 'therefore' (12.1) – if this is what God has done for us, then this is how we should live for him.

All too often we get the order wrong, and think that we need to do things before God will truly accept us. Or we miss out on part two, thinking that if God has done it all, what is there for us to do? But, like the pack of cards, if parts are missing then the whole thing is spoilt.

We can wake from sleep (13.11) since Jesus made us alive by his Spirit. We can walk in the light, since by Jesus' death and resurrection the powers of darkness have been defeated. We can 'put off' our natural selfish desires, since we have been baptized into Jesus' death and new life. In view of all that God has done, now is the time to live out the reality of his truth.

Prayer

Father, thank you for all you have done for me. Grant me the grace to rest in this.

Father, thank you for the way you call me to live. Grant me the life to live your truth.

Monday 4 December

Psalm 54

Save me, O God, by your name,
  and vindicate me by your might.
Hear my prayer, O God;
  give ear to the words of my mouth.

For the insolent have risen against me,
  the ruthless seek my life;
  they do not set God before them. (*Selah*)

But surely, God is my helper;
  the LORD is the upholder of my life.
He will repay my enemies for their evil.
  In your faithfulness, put an end to them.

With a freewill-offering I will sacrifice to you;
  I will give thanks to your name, O LORD, for it is good.
For he has delivered me from every trouble,
  and my eye has looked in triumph on my enemies.

What will your focus be?

This Psalm was written at time when David was being pursued by 'men without regard for God' – the men of King Saul. Saul's jealousy drove him to relentlessly pursue David, with the intention of killing him. David seeks refuge in the desert land of the Ziphites but, when they discover his whereabouts, they betray him to Saul (see 1 Samuel 23).

At first glance, it may be difficult to relate to David's experience – thankfully, I have never been pursued by an army! However, I have experienced problems that do not seem to want to go away, problems that resurface with tiresome regularity. Like David who experienced the betrayal of the Ziphites, I also know what it feels like to be let down by others.

Psalm 54 shows the way in which David responds to the pain and struggle of this situation. He is honest about what is happening to him, but he does not dwell upon the problems. Rather, David responds by *choosing* to focus on God. Trusting in what he knows to be true about God, he is able to pray with boldness, 'Save me . . . Vindicate me . . . Hear my prayer.' In 54.4 and 5, he proclaims God to be the one who helps and sustains him, the God of justice to whom he cries for deliverance. Ultimately, in the midst of difficulty, David is able to offer praise to God knowing that he is the same during bad times or good (54.6).

And so, for us, when we are faced with times of difficulty, we have a choice: we can focus on our problems; or we can focus on God. As we choose to look to God, although the situation may not immediately change, God can bring about a change within us. In the midst of difficulty we can discover him as the one who helps and sustains us, the faithful one who will act with justice.

Prayer

Father God, within difficult times
    please help me not to focus upon the problems,
but to choose to focus upon you,
    the author and the perfector of my faith. Amen.

Tuesday 5 December

Isaiah 43.1–7

But now thus says the LORD,
    he who created you, O Jacob,
    he who formed you, O Israel:
Do not fear, for I have redeemed you;
    I have called you by name, you are mine.
When you pass through the waters, I will be with you;
    and through the rivers, they shall not overwhelm you;
when you walk through fire you shall not be burned,
    and the flame shall not consume you.
For I am the LORD your God,
    the Holy One of Israel, your Saviour.
I give Egypt as your ransom,
    Ethiopia and Seba in exchange for you.
Because you are precious in my sight,
    and honoured, and I love you,
I give people in return for you,
    nations in exchange for your life.
Do not fear, for I am with you;
    I will bring your offspring from the east,
    and from the west I will gather you;
I will say to the north, 'Give them up,'
    and to the south, 'Do not withhold;
bring my sons from far away
    and my daughters from the end of the earth –
everyone who is called by my name,
    whom I created for my glory,
    whom I formed and made.'

Keep it simple

What can I give him, poor as I am?
If I were a shepherd, I would bring a lamb;
If I were a wise man, I would do my part.
Yet what I can I give him: give my heart.

(Christina Rossetti)

Christmas seems to start earlier every year and become more and more focused on buying presents and other goodies to help celebrate this season. The pressure mounts up to make this year's festivities better and more memorable than last year. In the stress and busyness it is good to take time out and to focus on the true meaning of the season. Advent is a time of preparation for the coming of the greatest gift of God to us, his Son Jesus.

As we prepare to celebrate this Christmas and remember the birth of Jesus, what do we think God wants in return from us? As Christina Rossetti implies in her hymn 'In the Bleak Mid-winter', the best gift we can bring to God is our heart.

If you struggle to believe that God is really interested and cares for you then look at today's passage from Isaiah and read the words as God's promise to you, 'Fear not for I have redeemed you, I have summoned you by name, you are mine.' Notice in the following verses that God's presence with you does not always mean an easy ride. But notice too that through the difficult times God 'will be with you' (Isaiah 43.2).

Maybe you are feeling under pressure, overwhelmed or stressed out at this time. Take hold of the fact that God cares for you and promises to be with you through the bad times as well as the good. Know that you are precious and honoured in God's sight, and he cares for you (Isaiah 43.4). And this Christmas try to keep it simple and bring the concerns of your heart before God.

Prayer

Father God, help me to keep my celebrations simple this Christmas and bring to you the gift you most desire – my heart. Amen.

Wednesday 6 December

Revelation 21.1–8

Then I saw a new heaven and a new earth; for the first heaven and the first earth had passed away, and the sea was no more. And I saw the holy city, the new Jerusalem, coming down out of heaven from God, prepared as a bride adorned for her husband. And I heard a loud voice from the throne saying,

'See, the home of God is among mortals.
He will dwell with them;
they will be his peoples,
and God himself will be with them;
he will wipe every tear from their eyes.
Death will be no more;
mourning and crying and pain will be no more,
for the first things have passed away.'

And the one who was seated on the throne said, 'See, I am making all things new.' Also he said, 'Write this, for these words are trustworthy and true.' Then he said to me, 'It is done! I am the Alpha and the Omega, the beginning and the end. To the thirsty I will give water as a gift from the spring of the water of life. Those who conquer will inherit these things, and I will be their God and they will be my children. But as for the cowardly, the faithless, the polluted, the murderers, the fornicators, the sorcerers, the idolaters, and all liars, their place will be in the lake that burns with fire and sulphur, which is the second death.'

The times they are a-changing

It is difficult to imagine a world in which there is no death or mourning or crying or pain, a world unchangingly good, eternally alive and unendingly joyful.

C. S. Lewis writes of the human condition that our 'bodies, passions and imaginations are in continual change, for to be in time means to change'. We know the passage of the seasons, that our summer gardens must die away in autumn, to bloom again in spring. We know the joy of good times tinged with sadness, and our darkest times shot through with moments of light and hope. In our lives as disciples we know periods of richness, life and growth alternating with periods of numbness, dryness and failure.

But God will 'make everything new', no longer under the tyranny of time, change and decay. These words are trustworthy and true – they are as true now as they will be when they are carried out. It is this knowledge that transforms the way we live now. When God does 'make everything new' it will not be by destruction and re-creation, but by renewing and transforming what already exists.

That makes this life and this world, all we are and do, significant. We are to persevere through change, through peaks and troughs, in the knowledge that God will refine and perfect all that we do to honour him.

Reflection

What changes am I facing in the coming weeks or months? How can I stay focused on what is of unchanging importance through this? What do I need to ask God for as I face this?

Thursday 7 December

Revelation 21.9–21

Then one of the seven angels who had the seven bowls full of the seven last plagues came and said to me, 'Come, I will show you the bride, the wife of the Lamb.' And in the spirit he carried me away to a great, high mountain and showed me the holy city Jerusalem coming down out of heaven from God. It has the glory of God and a radiance like a very rare jewel, like jasper, clear as crystal. It has a great, high wall with twelve gates, and at the gates twelve angels, and on the gates are inscribed the names of the twelve tribes of the Israelites; on the east three gates, on the north three gates, on the south three gates, and on the west three gates. And the wall of the city has twelve foundations, and on them are the twelve names of the twelve apostles of the Lamb.

The angel who talked to me had a measuring rod of gold to measure the city and its gates and walls. The city lies foursquare, its length the same as its width; and he measured the city with his rod, fifteen hundred miles; its length and width and height are equal. He also measured its wall, one hundred forty-four cubits by human measurement, which the angel was using. The wall is built of jasper, while the city is pure gold, clear as glass. The foundations of the wall of the city are adorned with every jewel; the first was jasper, the second sapphire, the third agate, the fourth emerald, the fifth onyx, the sixth carnelian, the seventh chrysolite, the eighth beryl, the ninth topaz, the tenth chrysoprase, the eleventh jacinth, the twelfth amethyst. And the twelve gates are twelve pearls, each of the gates is a single pearl, and the street of the city is pure gold, transparent as glass.

The triumph of grace

Have you ever seen a 'blue plaque' on a building? It usually com-memorates someone famous who lived there. I have often wondered what it would be like to see my own name on such a plaque.

Imagine being an ordinary Galilean fisherman, and reading that your name is written on the foundation of the Eternal City (21.14)! It is a sign of extraordinary grace – just think of the all-too-human depiction of the apostles in the Gospels – in a chapter overflowing with grace. It is no accident that it is one of the angels who had dispensed the plagues of judgement who now acts as tour-guide to the pinnacle of God's graciousness. It is grace, not judgement, which has the final word.

This whole chapter is like a multi-faceted jewel of grace, where almost every biblical expression of hope finds its fulfilment one way or another. The perfection of Eden, the mysterious encounter with the God of the tabernacle in the desert wanderings, the focus on the temple with its destruction and restoration, the hope of the nations, the power of kings – all find their fulfilment here. And it draws together all the themes that have come earlier in this book and shows the triumph of grace. The nations who have raged against the Lord's anointed now walk by the city's light. The kings of the earth, who worshipped the beast and adored the harlot, now bring their glory.

> I cannot tell how he will win the nations,
> how he will claim his earthly heritage,
> how satisfy the needs and aspirations
> of east and west, of sinner and of sage.
>
> (William Young Fullerton)

We cannot always know *how* God's grace will triumph – but we can be sure that it will.

Reflect

What are your needs and aspirations? Have you realized that God satisfies them all with his grace? What are the needs and aspirations of those around you? How can you help them realize that God will satisfy them too?

Friday 8 December

Isaiah 44.9–17

All who make idols are nothing, and the things they delight in do not profit; their witnesses neither see nor know. And so they will be put to shame. Who would fashion a god or cast an image that can do no good? Look, all its devotees shall be put to shame; the artisans too are merely human. Let them all assemble, let them stand up; they shall be terrified, they shall all be put to shame.

The blacksmith fashions it and works it over the coals, shaping it with hammers, and forging it with his strong arm; he becomes hungry and his strength fails, he drinks no water and is faint. The carpenter stretches a line, marks it out with a stylus, fashions it with planes, and marks it with a compass; he makes it in human form, with human beauty, to be set up in a shrine. He cuts down cedars or chooses a holm tree or an oak and lets it grow strong among the trees of the forest. He plants a cedar and the rain nourishes it. Then it can be used as fuel. Part of it he takes and warms himself; he kindles a fire and bakes bread. Then he makes a god and worships it, makes it a carved image and bows down before it. Half of it he burns in the fire; over this half he roasts meat, eats it and is satisfied. He also warms himself and says, 'Ah, I am warm, I can feel the fire!' The rest of it he makes into a god, his idol, bows down to it and worships it; he prays to it and says, 'Save me, for you are my god!'

No false dawns

Our culture drools worship at every angle: made-to fade Abercrombie sips Lambrini and kisses on both cheeks, drunk on power and status. Less than a mile away in the concrete jungle, hoodies sporting Towser-doggs and white gold smoke weed, conceal knives, idolizing 50-cent. Saturday comes and 42,000 sing glory and praise in orchestrated unison to eleven men and several patches of sewn leather – while the 'other half' flock to cathedrals-of-more, sacrificing on the altar of consumption . . . **STOP. SWITCH SCENE:**

Our culture drools worship at every angle. Is condemnation justified? Should a Christian speak the truth in love – prophetically discerning idolatry and folly? Surely 'all who make idols are nothing'. Yet, cultural rejection is already reaping Christian marginalization. Perhaps idolatry reveals a divine imprint? Or maybe the 'false dawn' of ill-targeted worship unveils an inherent eternal longing? **STOP. SCRIPTURE:**

The error of idolization is plainly unpacked in Isaiah 44, and forebodingly warned against: 'All its devotees shall be put to shame' (44.11). God's jealousy and desire for adulation from his chosen people burns fiercely, almost menacingly. But in isolation we miss the depth of compassion and grace poured out from the Almighty prior to these verses – the calling of Israel as his 'chosen' (44.1), the promise of protection (44.2) and the bestowal of purpose (44.8) precede this plea for faithfulness. **STOP. REALITY . . .**

As our culture exercises its worship-muscle, any Christian notion of condemnation must mutate into loving invitation – invitation for a people who 'do not know, nor . . . comprehend' (44.18) – invitation to Yahweh, to identity, destiny and purpose, through the mercy and welcome of Jesus Christ.

As we meditate on the demonstration of love outpoured in the divine Christmas child, the opportunity to respond beckons us, as it did the wise men and shepherds that 'holy night': to kneel in reverence before the Lord of history, now present among us, allowing the heavenly song of worship genetically planted within all humanity to burst forth . . . **WITHOUT STOPPING**

Saturday 9 December

Psalm 23

The LORD is my shepherd, I shall not want.
   He makes me lie down in green pastures;
he leads me beside still waters;
   he restores my soul.
He leads me in right paths
   for his name's sake.

Even though I walk through the darkest valley,
   I fear no evil;
for you are with me;
   your rod and your staff –
   they comfort me.

You prepare a table before me
   in the presence of my enemies;
you anoint my head with oil;
   my cup overflows.
Surely goodness and mercy shall follow me
   all the days of my life,
and I shall dwell in the house of the LORD
   my whole life long.

The song of the sheep

How bizarre that a Psalm should be written from the perspective of a sheep! Yet certainly Psalm 23.1–4 appears to be. And what more could a sheep want? Green pastures where it can feed, rest, spend time with its flock and family; quiet waters, where it can be washed and refreshed; and paths that are right and good.

Yet the sheep finds itself in the valley of the shadow of death, where there are wolves and snakes; the land is parched and rugged and the weather is wild. It is not frightened, because its shepherd is there with it, comforting it. Comforting it with a rod and staff? It is the rod with which the shepherd beats away the predator, and it is the staff which catches the sheep around its neck, and pulls it away from the edges, and back into the fold. It is a sheep who truly trusts its shepherd that can describe such action as comfort!

And perhaps there is more comfort still, in the hope of a table mountain, rich in grass, where it can be anointed with oil – where tics and mites can be treated, and where wounds can be cleansed and healed.

Prayer

Lord Jesus, my shepherd,

I find I have a lot in common with this sheep! You have provided me with the comfort of food, rest and refreshment. And yet sometimes I am in uncomfortable places. Sometimes I have taken myself there. And sometimes you have led me there. Please help me to trust your guidance and your discipline, so that I may find comfort in your presence wherever I am, and always look forward to the anointing of your love and goodness. Amen.

This reflection is inspired by Phillip Keller's book, *The Shepherd Trilogy*

Sunday 10 December

Psalm 8

O LORD, our Sovereign,
    how majestic is your name in all the earth!

You have set your glory above the heavens.
    Out of the mouths of babes and infants
you have founded a bulwark because of your foes,
    to silence the enemy and the avenger.

When I look at your heavens, the work of your fingers,
    the moon and the stars that you have established;
what are human beings that you are mindful of them,
    mortals that you care for them?

Yet you have made them a little lower than God,
    and crowned them with glory and honour.
You have given them dominion over the works of your hands;
    you have put all things under their feet,
all sheep and oxen,
    and also the beasts of the field,
the birds of the air, and the fish of the sea,
    whatever passes along the paths of the seas.

Smallness and greatness

When I was at primary school one of the ways my parents entertained me during those long holidays was to have day trips to London. On one of these my Dad took me to the (now sadly defunct) London Planetarium. For those not familiar with planetarium, you enter a large circular space and lie in seats that recline towards the dome-like ceiling. Then the lights go out, and all you can see are representations of the planets and constellations of stars in the night sky, with a commentary telling you what they all are, how far away they are, and so on.

Ever since that visit I have been fascinated by the night sky. On clear nights, I will often take a look upwards to see the stars and marvel at the size and beauty of the universe – and at the size and beauty of God and his creation. It is easy in these moments to feel overawed by it all, to feel insignificant and to wonder how God, with all the vastness of creation to look after, could be concerned with little and really rather ordinary-looking me.

Psalm 8 reassures, however. Feeling small and insignificant before the majesty of God and his creation is quite healthy. But God does not want us to dwell on it – after all, he made us only a little lower than heavenly beings, crowned us with glory and honour and made us ruler over the works of his hands! We are highly valuable and loved by God as his creation and as those in charge of his creation – the ultimate expression of this value being the sacrifice of Jesus on the cross to enable us to be counted as his precious children.

Reflection

Consider all the animals on the earth, all the birds in the air, all the fish in the sea, the moon and planets and all the stars in the sky. Think about the fact that God counts you as more valuable than all of this and that he has made you ruler of it.

How, knowing this, can you respond to God, both in prayer and practically?

Monday 11 December

Psalm 44.17–26

All this has come upon us,
    yet we have not forgotten you,
    or been false to your covenant.
Our heart has not turned back,
    nor have our steps departed from your way,
yet you have broken us in the haunt of jackals,
    and covered us with deep darkness.

If we had forgotten the name of our God,
    or spread out our hands to a strange god,
would not God discover this?
    For he knows the secrets of the heart.
Because of you we are being killed all day long,
    and accounted as sheep for the slaughter.

Rouse yourself! Why do you sleep, O LORD?
    Awake, do not cast us off for ever!
Why do you hide your face?
    Why do you forget our affliction and oppression?
For we sink down to the dust;
    our bodies cling to the ground.
Rise up, come to our help.
    Redeem us for the sake of your steadfast love.

Blessings and suffering

The Psalm begins with joyful memories of all the good things that God has done for the Psalmist. Take a moment now to reflect upon all the blessings that you have experienced in your life – supportive friends and family, prayers answered, the beauty of God's creation.

The Psalm then turns to the present, and it is a present of suffering, of feeling that God has rejected them, of disgrace. As we face times of suffering in our lives, times when we feel far from God, it is comforting to know that the Psalmist also felt this way. And we can learn from the Psalmist and know that it is all right to bring our complaint to God, to be truthful with God about how we feel.

Furthermore, the Psalmist continues by explaining that he cannot see a reason for this suffering. In verse 17 he writes, 'we have not forgotten you (God)'. The people had continued to be faithful to God, but this time of difficulty had still come. This question of why suffering happens continues to perplex us today. However, accepting that there will be times of trouble, we see in verse 23 that there is hope during these times.

There is hope that we can call upon God to support us through these times. As Christians in Advent we look again to the time when that hope becomes concrete as Jesus comes to Earth who is also called Emmanuel – God with us.

Prayer

Spend some time praying for those you know personally who are going through hard times, and for those places in the world experiencing difficulty.

Tuesday 12 December

Isaiah 46.8–13

Remember this and consider,
   recall it to mind, you transgressors,
   remember the former things of old;
for I am God, and there is no other;
   I am God, and there is no one like me,
declaring the end from the beginning
   and from ancient times things not yet done,
saying, 'My purpose shall stand,
   and I will fulfill my intention,'
calling a bird of prey from the east,
   the man for my purpose from a far country.
I have spoken, and I will bring it to pass;
   I have planned, and I will do it.
Listen to me, you stubborn of heart,
   you who are far from deliverance:
I bring near my deliverance, it is not far off,
   and my salvation will not tarry;
I will put salvation in Zion, for Israel my glory.

I will bring salvation soon

Recently I met someone who had spent twenty hours waiting outside a conference centre in order to audition for the TV reality series *Big Brother*. She spent the night outside, such was her desperation to be famous. Thousands each year go to extreme lengths for the chance to appear on similar reality TV shows in the hope of achieving fame.

Many people in society become obsessive about achieving fame, or wealth, or that better job. Yet such things become such an obsession that they begin to dominate the person's own life, and relationships with family and friends begin to suffer. The obsession becomes an idol which ends up being a burden on the person.

Yet Isaiah points out in today's reading that unlike idols, which become a burden, God cares for us and carries us. In fact, verse 9 reminds us that God is the *only* one who cares for us and can carry us – in contrast to the false idols. This culminates in God promising in verse 13 that 'I will bring salvation soon' even when the Israelites still fall for false idols and doubt God.

This is a time when we as Christians look to God bringing salvation soon through the coming of Jesus who is the one who frees us from sin, carries our burdens and cares for us. But we need to choose whether we are going to persevere with our old idols which are a constant burden to us, or to come to Jesus who offers to bear our burdens and care for us.

Reflection

What are the idols of the past that we are still living with? What does it involve for us to turn from them to the living God?

Wednesday 13 December

Psalm 34.1–10

I will bless the LORD at all times;
    his praise shall continually be in my mouth.
My soul makes its boast in the Lord;
    let the humble hear and be glad.
O magnify the LORD with me,
    and let us exalt his name together.

I sought the LORD, and he answered me,
    and delivered me from all my fears.
Look to him, and be radiant;
    so your faces shall never be ashamed.
This poor soul cried, and was heard by the LORD,
    and was saved from every trouble.
The angel of the LORD encamps
    around those who fear him, and delivers them.
O taste and see that the LORD is good;
    happy are those who take refuge in him.
O fear the LORD, you his holy ones,
    for those who fear him have no want.
The young lions suffer want and hunger,
    but those who seek the LORD lack no good thing.

The surprise of roast chicken

Open your mouth and taste, open your eyes and see.

How would you describe roast chicken? Other food is supposed to taste like chicken, from frogs' legs to crocodile meat, but what does chicken taste like? I guess it depends on which bit you are eating – but how would you paint a picture with words that shows what chicken tastes like, perhaps to someone who had never experienced it?

The only way to taste chicken is to open your mouth, tear off a piece of meat and chew, taking your time to notice which bit of your tongue is stimulated by it. Have you added salt to bring the flavour out, and is this now masking the taste of your chicken? Can you separate the chicken taste from the marinade, or lemon, or bay leaf you have cooked it with?

Often we sit and look at God, we describe him to friends, and then it is as if we are eating fast food – life is busy and there is no time to hang around – and we rush the experience of tasting God. We can taste God through the gifts he gives us, the people we meet, the creation around us and of course the food he provides for us.

Take some time to think about an aspect of God. Our taste of God is affected by our parenting experiences, our teaching as children, our culture and expectations of God and life and others. God is good; notice the parts of your life that have been stimulated by this aspect of God, and enjoy, take your time, and then share it with someone else.

Prayer

Father God, thank you for the ways that I have tasted your goodness. Grant me the grace to take time to taste afresh today. Amen.

Thursday 14 December

Psalm 37.1–7, 34–36

Do not fret because of the wicked;
  do not be envious of wrongdoers,
for they will soon fade like the grass,
  and wither like the green herb.

Trust in the LORD, and do good;
  so you will live in the land, and enjoy security.
Take delight in the LORD,
  and he will give you the desires of your heart.

Commit your way to the LORD;
  trust in him, and he will act.
He will make your vindication shine like the light,
  and the justice of your cause like the noonday.

Be still before the LORD, and wait patiently for him;
  do not fret over those who prosper in their way,
over those who carry out evil devices.

Wait for the LORD, and keep to his way,
  and he will exalt you to inherit the land;
  you will look on the destruction of the wicked.

I have seen the wicked oppressing,
  and towering like a cedar of Lebanon.
Again I passed by, and they were no more;
  though I sought them, they could not be found.

Restoring hope

I met Andrew when he was crippled with anxiety and depression. He had been with his company for some time and used to love his job. However, things had changed and he was no longer able to meet expectations because of his disability. Andrew had always done the right thing, giving his best in any situation. Recognizing his problems, he approached his supervisor to ask for help.

Many people can identify with this type of situation, where you fear, or know, you are being left behind in a changing world. Andrew was in a vulnerable position as he faced up to his value in society being a disabled man approaching fifty. However, although stressful, this was not the cause of his brokenness and despair. It was the reaction of his supervisor. Andrew was not asked to leave but was offered assistance. On the surface, it appeared the company was making every effort to accommodate his disability. In reality, there was a hidden campaign of bullying and humiliation, masterminded to make Andrew resign. The company started disciplinary proceedings against him, and as the pressure mounted Andrew felt more and more isolated and dehumanized. Andrew had done the right thing but now felt robbed of his dignity as a result.

Sometimes, walking the path of righteousness leads you to very lonely and isolated places in your life, where even those you love dearly cannot see the sense in what you are doing. For Andrew, Psalm 37 tells him he will never be alone because he puts his faith and trust in God. It tells him not to worry when people succeed in their ways. It tells him God places a high value on him – and that, in the end, those who plan evil will come to nothing.

Reflection

In meditating on Psalm 37, let the words restore hope into any dark situation in which you find yourself and help you to rediscover that you are never alone when you commit your way to the Lord.

Friday 15 December

1 Thessalonians 4.1–12

Finally, brothers and sisters, we ask and urge you in the Lord Jesus that, as you learned from us how you ought to live and to please God (as, in fact, you are doing), you should do so more and more. For you know what instructions we gave you through the Lord Jesus. For this is the will of God, your sanctification: that you abstain from fornication; that each one of you knows how to control your own body in holiness and honour, not with lustful passion, like the Gentiles who do not know God; that no one wrongs or exploits a brother or sister in this matter, because the Lord is an avenger in all these things, just as we have already told you beforehand and solemnly warned you. For God did not call us to impurity but in holiness. Therefore whoever rejects this rejects not human authority but God, who also gives his Holy Spirit to you.

Now concerning love of the brothers and sisters, you do not need to have anyone write to you, for you yourselves have been taught by God to love one another; and indeed you do love all the brothers and sisters throughout Macedonia. But we urge you, beloved, to do so more and more, to aspire to live quietly, to mind your own affairs, and to work with your hands, as we directed you, so that you may behave properly toward outsiders and be dependent on no one.

Building with bananas

Years ago I read a Christian book by Derek Copley called *Building with Bananas*. The title came from an overheard conversation on a building site involving a bricklayer standing next to a pile of badly made bricks. Looking at the curved-up ends he muttered, 'How can anyone expect me to build with these? They're just like bananas!' Derek Copley made the point that in spite of the odd-shaped bricks, the bricklayer managed to use his skill and build a fine wall.

God does the same with us. In spite of our weaknesses and imperfections he longs to build us into a people who show his glory in the world, and that is the message in this passage. Here, Paul uses words like 'holy' and 'sanctified' (4.3, 4.4 and 4.7), which sound as if they describe a super-class Christian living in a monastery or captured for all time in a stained-glass window. In fact, these words are about a life being built by the Holy Spirit to live God's way in a tough world.

This passage says some important things about being holy.

First, being or becoming holy is not optional – it is God's plan for all Christians (4.3) who are called to live lives that please God, with the help of his Holy Spirit.

Second, holiness involves being transformed in the way we live as sexual beings (4.3–8). Sexuality is fundamental to being human but it is not to be used to exploit or harm others. This involves respecting one's marriage partner as someone made in God's image – not treating him or her as an object for selfish gratification.

Third, holiness involves loving actions toward both Christians and non-Christians (4.9 and 4.12). In other words, holiness is practical and shows itself in costly actions that benefit others.

Fourth, holiness finds expression in our willingness to work or serve diligently; and finally it's about minding your own business – not getting into gossip (4.11).

In other words, holiness involves living down-to-earth lives – God's way – conscious of the coming of the Lord. How's it going?

Saturday 16 December

Psalm 42.1–5

As a deer longs for flowing streams,
    so my soul longs for you, O God.
My soul thirsts for God,
    for the living God.
When shall I come and behold
    the face of God?
My tears have been my food
    day and night,
while people say to me continually,
    'Where is your God?'

These things I remember,
    as I pour out my soul:
how I went with the throng,
    and led them in procession to the house of God,
with glad shouts and songs of thanksgiving,
    a multitude keeping festival.
Why are you cast down, O my soul,
    and why are you disquieted within me?
Hope in God; for I shall again praise him,
    my help and my God.

Age-old challenges

Although this Psalm is about the suffering experienced by the Psalmist during the exile of the Jews, we can take comfort in the knowledge that even as far back as when the Psalmist was writing, non-believers still questioned the existence of God (42.1–3), 'church' attendance was experiencing a low point (42.4–5) and occasionally doubt lingered in believers' minds about the presence of God in their lives (42.9–10).

These are problems that are similar to some of the problems faced by Christians in the modern world. All of us at some point in our lives feel that God has forsaken us or forgotten about us, but we can take comfort in the words of the Psalmist and knowing that even our Saviour, Jesus Christ, cried out, 'Eli, Eli, lama sabachthani?' ('My God, my God, why have you forsaken me?'). We should always remember that no matter how bad our lives, God is always present in our lives and he has not forsaken us. He has brought us eternal life through the death of his only Son, Jesus Christ.

Prayer

Lord God, we thank you for all that you have done for us to make our lives enjoyable and fulfilling. We also remember that pain and suffering are both part of our lives. We pray that your presence will be felt not only during times of great joy but also as a source of relief from the trials and sufferings of all your children's lives. We pray for all those experiencing suffering and grief and that you may be with them at this time of difficulty. Amen.

Sunday 17 December

Isaiah 25.1–9

O LORD, you are my God;
I will exalt you, I will praise your name;
for you have done wonderful things,
    plans formed of old, faithful and sure.
For you have made the city a heap,
    the fortified city a ruin;
the palace of aliens is a city no more,
    it will never be rebuilt.
Therefore strong peoples will glorify you;
    cities of ruthless nations will fear you.
For you have been a refuge to the poor,
    a refuge to the needy in their distress,
    a shelter from the rainstorm and a shade from the heat.
When the blast of the ruthless was like a winter rainstorm,
    the noise of aliens like heat in a dry place,
you subdued the heat with the shade of clouds;
    the song of the ruthless was stilled.

On this mountain the LORD of hosts will make for all peoples
    a feast of rich food, a feast of well-aged wines,
    of rich food filled with marrow, of well-aged wines strained clear.
And he will destroy on this mountain
    the shroud that is cast over all peoples,
    the sheet that is spread over all nations;
    he will swallow up death for ever.
Then the LORD God will wipe away the tears from all faces,
    and the disgrace of his people he will take away from all the earth,
    for the LORD has spoken.
It will be said on that day,
    Lo, this is our God; we have waited for him, so that he might
        save us.
    This is the LORD for whom we have waited;
    let us be glad and rejoice in his salvation.

Amazing and faithful

> You have done amazing things,
>> you have faithfully carried out the plans you made long ago.

(Isaiah 25.1, CEV)

A friend told me how her son really wanted a pet for Christmas, so a rabbit and guinea-pig were duly bought and hidden in the garage. On Christmas Eve a drink was left for Santa and a carrot for Rudolph and the children went to bed. A note was tied to the carrot saying, 'Rudolph has had lots of carrots but I think you'll need this for what I've left you in your garage.' On Christmas morning the child saw this and was asked by his mother what he thought was waiting for him and replied, 'He's got me what I've always wanted. He's got me a reindeer!'

In the manner of young children, the disappointment of not having a reindeer was soon gone in the face of the delight he had in his new pets. For us, we can see how a guinea-pig was far more suited to him than a reindeer would have been!

Christmas is always stressful, with countless pressures on us from quite early on in the season. There is pressure to find the right gifts, prepare the right food in the right way and so on. This passage of praise to God reminds us that, whatever our current stress or concern, he has prepared good things for us – and his judgement of what we really need (like most parents) is always better than ours. More than this, he has done amazing things for us!

Reflection

In the midst of the Christmas bustle, take a moment to stop and take pleasure in the good things God has already given you. Ask him for his perspective on everything going on around you.

Monday 18 December

Isaiah 49.14–21

But Zion said, 'The LORD has forsaken me,
    my LORD has forgotten me.'
Can a woman forget her nursing-child,
    or show no compassion for the child of her womb?
Even these may forget,
    yet I will not forget you.
See, I have inscribed you on the palms of my hands;
    your walls are continually before me.
Your builders outdo your destroyers,
    and those who laid you waste go away from you.
Lift up your eyes all around and see;
    they all gather, they come to you.
As I live, says the LORD,
    you shall put all of them on like an ornament,
    and like a bride you shall bind them on.

Surely your waste and your desolate places
    and your devastated land –
surely now you will be too crowded for your inhabitants,
    and those who swallowed you up will be far away.
The children born in the time of your bereavement
    will yet say in your hearing:
'The place is too crowded for me;
    make room for me to settle.'
Then you will say in your heart,
    'Who has borne me these?
I was bereaved and barren,
    exiled and put away –
    so who has reared these?
I was left all alone –
    where then have these come from?'

Straightening things out

When we think of today's world, we could be forgiven for thinking that there is no hope – that God really has forsaken us. As we watch the news we are bombarded by stories of tensions, by images of war-torn countries. We see the innocent victims caught in the midst of violence and war and we ask ourselves whether we might ever see the realities of peace. We live in a world that is tense with aggression and distorted with selfishness.

In the Isaiah passage we read that the people of Israel felt that God had forsaken them in Babylon. Isaiah, however, points out that God would never forget them, as a loving mother would not forget her little child. We learn that God's promises will always be fulfilled. Just as God had done as he promised at the time of the exodus, so he would do it again when the exiles returned to Israel. It is on the fulfilment of these promises that we must base our hope for the future, our hope for a peaceful world. Where before what seemed impossible was realized, we must believe that God can again do the seemingly impossible.

Our God is faithful. However, there may be times when we have to wait to see the realities of his promises being fulfilled. Psalm 40 (another of the lectionary readings for today) shows us that while waiting for God to help is not always easy, there will be benefits in the end. David is greatly blessed after his trial of waiting.

Our hope, then, stems from God's faithfulness. We have to believe that God's faithfulness boasts more than mere humans can understand, and that his promises are irrevocable. As it is written in Galatians 5.5: 'Through the Spirit, by faith, we eagerly wait for the hope of righteousness.'

Prayer

Heavenly Father, help us in this time of waiting for justice and peace to focus on your faithfulness, and on the hope that stems from the knowledge that your promises will always be fulfilled. Amen.

Tuesday 19 December

1 Thessalonians 5.12–28

But we appeal to you, brothers and sisters, to respect those who labour among you, and have charge of you in the Lord and admonish you; esteem them very highly in love because of their work. Be at peace among yourselves. And we urge you, beloved, to admonish the idlers, encourage the faint-hearted, help the weak, be patient with all of them. See that none of you repays evil for evil, but always seek to do good to one another and to all. Rejoice always, pray without ceasing, give thanks in all circumstances; for this is the will of God in Christ Jesus for you. Do not quench the Spirit. Do not despise the words of prophets, but test everything; hold fast to what is good; abstain from every form of evil.

May the God of peace himself sanctify you entirely; and may your spirit and soul and body be kept sound and blameless at the coming of our Lord Jesus Christ. The one who calls you is faithful, and he will do this.

Beloved, pray for us.

Greet all the brothers and sisters with a holy kiss. I solemnly command you by the Lord that this letter be read to all of them.

The grace of our Lord Jesus Christ be with you.

Beautiful anyway

At a first glance this passage looks like a 'to do' list, a group of personality traits we all need to achieve before Christmas – a group of traits that it is impossible to imagine one person holding. It seems to be about watching and changing our conduct, while at the same time watching and encouraging (or not) the conduct of others. Still we struggle and strive to find perfection in ourselves. My favourite verses are 23–24, not surprisingly, because they shift the emphasis from ourselves to our creator, the 'God of peace'. The Message version puts it like this:

> May God himself, the God who makes everything holy and whole, make you holy and whole, put you together – spirit, soul and body . . . (5.23)

So, where does this leave us? In this short passage we find a plea to be amazingly, totally un-humanly holy, and at the same time a promise that it is God who puts us together, and that he will perform this miracle within our topsy-turvy lives.

Nichole Nordeman explores this theme in her song 'Anyway'. She relates us to paintings that get grubby as we live our lives, and which we spend our time trying to clean. By doing this we cannot make ourselves something we are not, but we can get a glimpse of the original picture of holiness that God created. The chorus goes like this:

> But you called me beautiful,
> when you saw my shame,
> and you placed me on the wall,
> anyway.

Maybe that's the point. If God calls me beautiful, then what am I doing, trusting in my own polishing skills? The one who calls us is faithful, and he will do it. We just have to let him hang us on the wall.

Prayer

Thank you, Father, for the beauty you have created in my life and the lives of those around me. Help me see your beauty in others – and in my own life too. Amen.

Wednesday 20 December

Psalm 46

God is our refuge and strength,
    a very present help in trouble.
Therefore we will not fear, though the earth should change,
    though the mountains shake in the heart of the sea;
though its waters roar and foam,
    though the mountains tremble with its tumult. (*Selah*)

There is a river whose streams make glad the city of God,
    the holy habitation of the Most High.
God is in the midst of the city; it shall not be moved;
    God will help it when the morning dawns.
The nations are in an uproar, the kingdoms totter;
    he utters his voice, the earth melts.
The Lord of hosts is with us;
    the God of Jacob is our refuge. (*Selah*)

Come, behold the works of the Lord;
    see what desolations he has brought on the earth.
He makes wars cease to the end of the earth;
    he breaks the bow, and shatters the spear;
    he burns the shields with fire.
'Be still, and know that I am God!
    I am exalted among the nations,
    I am exalted in the earth.'
The Lord of hosts is with us;
    the God of Jacob is our refuge. (*Selah*)

Refuge and our strength

God is our refuge and our strength,
  a very present help in times of trouble.
                                    (Psalm 46.1)

Thank goodness this is the case! As the Psalm goes on, no matter how catastrophic things may be, God *is* our refuge and strength.

There is nothing like a disaster to focus our attention and make us realize how reliant we really are on God. If the house is struck by lightning, leaving a gaping hole in the roof, it reminds us of the power of the natural elements around us. If a baby is critically ill, it makes us aware of how vulnerable and precious life is. As we stand looking helplessly on, we are aware that the power and control we have is not really our power or control at all.

Time can appear to stand still as the rest of the world rages on around us. Yet it is at times like this that we can be most aware of God – the creator and sustainer of life. It can be a matter of will by which we declare our faith in God rather than the physical evidence before us. We can echo the Psalmist's words, and add our own, confident that God will hear us. In the moments when words fail or we are overcome by the magnitude of the situation we face, we can be still and know that God is God.

When the crisis passes we can look back and remember that the presence of God that was with us in the storm is still with us in the calm and the mundane. This awareness of God as our refuge and strength in troubled times can be recalled in times of peace and order as well. Then our natural response is to exalt the Lord our God in the knowledge that, through thick and thin, God, our refuge, is with us.

Thursday 21 December

Psalm 121

I lift up my eyes to the hills –
    from where will my help come?
My help comes from the Lord,
    who made heaven and earth.

He will not let your foot be moved;
    he who keeps you will not slumber.
He who keeps Israel
    will neither slumber nor sleep.

The Lord is your keeper;
    the Lord is your shade at your right hand.
The sun shall not strike you by day,
    nor the moon by night.

The Lord will keep you from all evil;
    he will keep your life.
The Lord will keep
    your going out and your coming in
    from this time on and for evermore.

Whom do you rely on?

The Lord shall keep you from all evil;
   it is he who shall keep your soul.

(Psalm 121.7)

In times of severe testing and trial, it is easy to turn to God as a last resort because there is nothing else we can do. Once we have exhausted all our other resources, that is the time when we find ourselves crying out to God, out of sheer desperation.

This is not the relationship God intends us to have with him. He desires to be more than the fourth emergency service, only called upon when all else fails. Do you only call upon God when your self-reliance has run its course?

God wants you to turn to him and rely on him for everything you do and everything you are. After all, he is your creator and he longs for you to know him intimately, because that is how he knows you.

The lifting up of the eyes is a confident and bold prayer-gesture indicative of a trusting heart. It is with a trusting heart that God wants you to accept those great blessings that the Psalm speaks of. In all you do, God faithfully watches over you, day and night. He does not rest for one moment. He loves you and protects you from danger. He sustains your life, body and soul in times of trial. He knows everything there is to know about you: your passions and sorrows; your joys and suffering. He will never forsake you; he lavishes his attention for eternity.

Reflection

If you place your reliance and trust in yourself or other people, turn now to God, having confidence in his faithfulness. Know that he is waiting to embrace you with open arms and show you a life of fullness, which comes from totally relying on him.

Friday 22 December

Psalm 124

If it had not been the LORD who was on our side
  – let Israel now say –
if it had not been the LORD who was on our side,
  when our enemies attacked us,
then they would have swallowed us up alive,
  when their anger was kindled against us;
then the flood would have swept us away,
  the torrent would have gone over us;
then over us would have gone
  the raging waters.

Blessed be the LORD,
  who has not given us
  as prey to their teeth.
We have escaped like a bird
  from the snare of the fowlers;
the snare is broken,
  and we have escaped.

Our help is in the name of the LORD,
  who made heaven and earth.

We live by faith, not by sight

Psalm 124 is a great psalm of thanksgiving for God's deliverance at a time of much danger and pressure. It is a realization that, 'Had it not been for the intervention of our great and mighty God, we would have been cooked!' Probably most of us can recollect occasions when God has been the difference between our coming through a testing situation or going under.

It is good to thank God as we look back on situations of stress that he has brought us through; what is a little more difficult is to trust him at the time we are, to use the imagery of this Psalm, in the midst of the battle. It is easy to thank God for what we can see he has done; not so easy to thank him for what he is going to do when we cannot see how he is going to do it!

Yet this is what faith is all about: 'being sure of what we hope for and certain of *what we do not see*' (Hebrews 11.1). And Paul reminds us that 'we live by faith, not by sight' (2 Corinthians 5.7). In other words, the normal Christian life is to believe God and thank him for what he has not yet done! It is as we do this and see God work in marvellous – and usually completely unexpected – ways that our faith grows and develops. This is the hope that transforms us: we become different people as we discover time and again that God is faithful.

If you are thinking, 'This is the kind of Christian life I would love to live – how do I get there?' then here is a thought to chew over: faith exercised in the hard times is the fruit of feeding on God's word in the good times.

Reflection

Am I cultivating my faith in God? Or am I expecting it just to be there when a crisis comes?

Saturday 23 December

Psalm 130

Out of the depths I cry to you, O LORD.
   LORD, hear my voice!
Let your ears be attentive
   to the voice of my supplications!

If you, O LORD, should mark iniquities,
   LORD, who could stand?
But there is forgiveness with you,
   so that you may be revered.

I wait for the LORD, my soul waits,
   and in his word I hope;
my soul waits for the LORD
   more than those who watch for the morning,
   more than those who watch for the morning.

O Israel, hope in the LORD!
   For with the LORD there is steadfast love,
   and with him is great power to redeem.
It is he who will redeem Israel
   from all its iniquities.

From depths to height

'It feels like I've hit rock bottom.' Most of us feel like this sometimes. Some of us feel like this a lot of the time. The Psalmists are realistic about how awful life can be, and this Psalm is a good example – it arises out of the depths (of despair).

The Psalm falls into four parts, each of which starts with a reference to the Lord: verses 1–2, 3–4, 5–6 and 7–8. Part one, typical of such 'lament' Psalms, opens with a cry to the Lord, twice pleading for God to hear the prayer. Part two acknowledges the seriousness of sin – if God took account of all our sins, all of us would be lost! However, it states with confidence that forgiveness is found in God.

Rather than talking to God, part three speaks about God, repeating several times that the Psalmist 'waits for' (or perhaps 'hopes in' – the words used may have this sense) God. Part four then calls on the community also to 'wait' for (or 'hope' in) God who will also redeem it from the consequences of its sins.

There really is hope in the depths of despair. That hope is not founded on ourselves, our circumstances or other people, but on the God who hears our cry and has the power to forgive and redeem, and who also demonstrates steadfast love – both for individuals and for communities.

Reflection

What have you discovered anew this Advent about God's love and the hope that he gives us? How does the message of Christmas express both the seriousness of sin and God's grace in forgiveness?

Sunday 24 December

Revelation 22.12–17

'See, I am coming soon; my reward is with me, to repay according to everyone's work. I am the Alpha and the Omega, the first and the last, the beginning and the end.'

Blessed are those who wash their robes, so that they will have the right to the tree of life and may enter the city by the gates. Outside are the dogs and sorcerers and fornicators and murderers and idolaters, and everyone who loves and practises falsehood.

'It is I, Jesus, who sent my angel to you with this testimony for the churches. I am the root and the descendant of David, the bright morning star.'

The Spirit and the bride say, 'Come.'
And let everyone who hears say, 'Come.'
And let everyone who is thirsty come.
Let anyone who wishes take the water of life as a gift.

Santa Claus is coming to town

One of my least favourite Christmas songs is 'Santa Claus is coming to town'. I'm not sure exactly why. Perhaps it is the relentless cheeriness of it; possibly it is the childish division of everyone into 'naughty' or 'nice'. I think a large part of it is the fact that the motivation held out for being good is the presents you might receive. I was seven years old when I first realized that my parents had finished their Christmas shopping by 19 December and so however I behaved after that probably would not affect what presents I got.

'Behold I am coming soon!' Advent tells us that Jesus is coming – first as a little child in Bethlehem, but also, ultimately, as the Alpha and the Omega, the Lord of all the universe. This passage assures us that there will be judgement, that there will be those who go 'into the city' and those who will 'remain outside' (22.14, 15). How should we respond?

We respond by accepting Jesus' free offer to us – not of presents and amusing toys like those we would find in a stocking, but of 'the free gift of the water of life' (22.17).

The challenge is not to make sure we are nice instead of naughty. The challenge is to take Jesus seriously as both the babe of Bethlehem and as the ruler of everything there is. The challenge is to accept the offer he holds out to 'whoever is thirsty, whoever wishes' and the offer to come. In accepting this offer, we will be transformed and we will go on being transformed.

Prayer

Jesus, you are coming soon. Help me to see more of who you really are. Help me to hope and trust in your free gift of life to me, and through this transform me into your likeness. Amen.

List of Contributors

Andy Mason
Vinny Whitworth
Ali Taylor
Julie Probert
Mark Griffiths
Ruth Whitworth
Jeremy Clack
Rupert Hankey
Doug Ingram
Ian Paul
Steve Taylor
Luke Dean
James Ogley
Ellie Clack
Tony Mitchell
Helen Jary
Chris Meyer
Paula Meyer
Rachel Hill-Brown
Daniel Cooke
James Di Castiglione
Steve Bailey
Angie Bailey
Sarah Giles